# How To Overcome With Depression

Chirstopher Carlson

ISBN: 9798464313514

# Contents

# ACKNOWLEDGMENTS

Sadness can be a difficult emotion to deal with, not only due to the pain it causes, but also because of the factors that caused the sadness in the first place. Sadness can be the result of loss, helplessness, or disappointment, among many other things. It is important to remember, though, that sadness is one of the most common and natural human emotions, and is something that will ultimately help us appreciate our happy times.

Sometimes, though, it is possible for sadness to deepen, and this may be a sign that you are suffering from a form of depression. If you feel as though you are increasingly sad, and feel like your sadness is difficult to explain, this information on depression may help.

# 1.WHAT IS DEPRESSION?

*What Is Depression?*

Depression is a disorder that is evidenced by excessive sadness, loss of interest in enjoyable things, and low motivation.

It is normal to experience feelings of sadness and despair in response to adverse life events. Such events could include loss, major life changes, stress, or disappointment.

In most cases, the sad feelings resolve as you come to terms with the changes in your life. In situations such as bereavement, these feelings may persist for months and return at significant times, such as birthdays and anniversaries related to the lost loved one.

Provided you have times when you can enjoy things, however, this sadness is not a sign of depression.

Depression is common. One in three people will experience a major depressive episode at some stage in their lives. While most cases of depression are mild, about one person in ten will have a moderate or severe episode.

*What Are The Signs Of Depression?*

The features of depression include:

**Psychological Symptoms:**

- Feeling miserable. This misery is present for much of the day but may vary in its intensity. The misery lasts for weeks.
- Loss of interest or pleasure in usual activities.
- Slowed or inefficient thinking with poor concentration, leading to difficulties sorting out problems or making plans or decisions.
- Recurring unpleasant thoughts, particularly about being guilty, being a bad and unworthy person,
- Thoughts that you would be better off dead or of harming yourself in some way.

**Physical Symptoms:**

- Loss of appetite with excessive loss of weight.
- Loss of interest in sex
- Loss of energy, even when not physically active.
- Loss of sleep despite feeling exhausted. Sleep is typically restless and unsatisfying with early morning wakening (one to two hours earlier than usual). Some people, however, may actually sleep a lot more than usual.
- Slowed activity and speech.

Any of these features may serve as warning signs of depression. You need to exhibit at least five of these symptoms to be suffering with a depressive disorder.

*What Causes Depression?*

**What Are the Main Causes of Depression?**

There are a number of factors that may increase the chance of depression, including the following:

- **Abuse.** Past physical, sexual, or emotional abuse can increase the vulnerability to clinical depression later in life.

- **Certain medications.** Some drugs, such as isotretinoin (used to treat acne), the antiviral drug interferon-alpha, and corticosteroids, can increase your risk of depression.

- **Conflict.** Depression in someone who has the biological vulnerability to develop depression may result from personal conflicts or disputes with family members or friends.

- **Death or a loss.** Sadness or grief from the death or loss of a loved one, though natural, may increase the risk of depression.

- **Genetics.** A family history of depression may increase the risk. It's thought that depression is a complex trait, meaning that there are probably many different genes that each exert small effects, rather than a single gene that contributes to disease risk. The genetics of depression, like most psychiatric disorders, are not as simple or straightforward as in *purely* genetic diseases such as Huntington's chorea or cystic fibrosis.

- **Major events.** Even good events such as starting a new job, graduating, or getting married can lead to depression. So can moving, losing a job or income, getting divorced, or retiring. However, the syndrome of clinical depression is never just a "normal" response to stressful life events.

- **Other personal problems.** Problems such as social isolation due to other mental illnesses or being cast out of a family or social group can contribute to the risk of developing clinical depression.

- **Serious illnesses.** Sometimes depression co-exists with a major illness or may be triggered by another medical condition.

- **Substance abuse.** Nearly 30% of people with substance abuse problems also have major or clinical depression. Even if drugs or alcohol temporarily make you feel better, they ultimately will aggravate depression.

**How Is Biology Related to Depression?**

Researchers have noted differences in the brains of people who have a clinical depression as compared to those who do not. For instance, the hippocampus, a small part of the brain that is vital to the storage of memories, appears to be smaller in some people with a history of depression than in those who've never been depressed.

A smaller hippocampus has fewer serotonin receptors. Serotonin is one of many brain chemicals known as neurotransmitters that allow communication across circuits that connect different brain regions involved in processing emotions.

Scientists do not know why the hippocampus may be smaller in some people with depression. Some researchers have found that the stress hormone cortisol is produced in excess in depressed people.

These investigators believe that cortisol has a toxic or "shrinking" effect on the development of hippocampus. Some experts theorize that depressed people are simply born with a smaller hippocampus and are therefore inclined to suffer from depression.

There are many other brain regions, and pathways between specific regions, thought to be involved with depression, and likely, no single brain structure or pathway fully accounts for clinical depression.

One thing is certain -- depression is a complex illness with many contributing factors. The latest scans and studies of brain structure and function suggest that antidepressants can exert what are called "neurotrophic effects," meaning that they can help sustain nerve cells, prevent them from dying, and allow them to form stronger connections that withstand biological stresses.

As scientists gain a better understanding of the causes of depression, health professionals will be able to make better "tailored" diagnoses and, in turn, prescribe more effective treatment plans.

**How Is Genetics Linked to the Risk of Depression?**

We know that depression can sometimes run in families. This suggests that there's at least a partial genetic link to depression. Children, siblings, and parents of people with severe depression are somewhat more likely to suffer from depression than are members of the general population.

Multiple genes interacting with one another in special ways probably contribute to the various types of depression that run in families.

Yet despite the evidence of a family link to depression, it is unlikely that there is a single "depression" gene, but rather, many genes that each contribute small effects toward depression when they interact with the environment.

**Can Certain Drugs Cause Depression**

In certain people, drugs may lead to depression. For example, medications such as barbiturates, benzodiazepines, and the acne drug isotretinoin (formerly sold as Accutane, now Absorica, Amnesteem, Claravis, Myorisan, Zenatane) have sometimes been associated with depression, especially in older people. Likewise, medications such as corticosteroids, opioids (codeine, morphine), and anticholinergics taken to relieve stomach cramping can sometimes cause changes and fluctuations in mood. Even blood pressure medications called beta-blockers have been linked to depression."

**What's the Link Between Depression and Chronic Illness?**

In some people, a chronic illness causes depression. A chronic illness is an illness that lasts for a very long time and usually cannot be cured completely.

However, chronic illnesses can often be controlled through diet, exercise, lifestyle habits, and certain medications. Some examples of chronic illnesses that may cause depression are diabetes, heart disease, arthritis, kidney disease, HIV/AIDS, lupus, and multiple sclerosis (MS). Hypothyroidism may also lead to depressed feelings.

Researchers believe that treating the depression may sometimes also help the co-existing medical illness improve.

### Is Depression Linked to Chronic Pain?

When pain lingers for weeks to months, it's referred to as being "chronic." Not only does chronic pain hurt, it also disturbs your sleep, your ability to exercise and be active, your relationships, and your productivity at work. Can you see how chronic pain may also leave you feeling sad, isolated, and depressed?

There is help for chronic pain and depression. A multifaceted program of medicine, psychotherapy, support groups, and more can help you manage your pain, ease your depression, and get your life back on track.

For in depth information, see Depression and Chronic Pain.

### Does Depression Often Occur With Grief?

Grief is a common, normal response to loss. Losses that may lead to grief include the death or separation of a loved one, loss of a job, death or loss of a beloved pet, or any number of other changes in life, such as divorce, becoming an "empty nester," or retirement.

Anyone can experience grief and loss, but not everyone will experience clinical depression, which differs from grief in that depression involves a range of other symptoms such as feelings of low self-worth, negative thoughts about the future, and suicide, whereas grief involves feelings of emptiness, loss and longing for a loved one, with an intact capacity to feel pleasure. Each person is unique in how he or she copes with these feelings.

# 2. COPING WITH DEPRESSION

When you're depressed, you can't just will yourself to "snap out of it." But these tips can help put you on the road to recovery.

Woman gazes wearily with sad eyes, lost in thought, chin resting on bent fingers of back of hand

*Why is dealing with depression so difficult?*

Depression drains your energy, hope, and drive, making it difficult to take the steps that will help you to feel better. Sometimes, just thinking about the things you should do to feel better, like exercising or spending time with friends, can seem exhausting or impossible to put into action.

It's the Catch-22 of depression recovery: The things that help the most are the things that are the most difficult to do. There is a big difference, however, between something that's difficult and something that's impossible.

While recovering from depression isn't quick or easy, you do have more control than you realize—even if your depression is severe and stubbornly persistent. The key is to start small and build from there. You may not have much energy, but by drawing on all your reserves, you should have enough to take a walk around the block or pick up the phone to call a loved one, for example.

Taking the first step is always the hardest. But going for a walk or getting up and dancing to your favorite music, for example, is something you can do right now.

And it can substantially boost your mood and energy for several hours—long enough to put a second recovery step into action, such as preparing a mood-boosting meal or arranging to meet an old friend. By taking the following small but positive steps day by day, you'll soon lift the heavy fog of depression and find yourself feeling happier, healthier, and more hopeful again.

**Coping with depression tip 1: Reach out and stay connected**

Getting support plays an essential role in overcoming depression. On your own, it can be difficult to maintain a healthy perspective and sustain the effort required to beat depression.

At the same time, the very nature of depression makes it difficult to reach out for help. When you're depressed, the tendency is to withdraw and isolate so that connecting to even close family members and friends can be tough.

You may feel too exhausted to talk, ashamed at your situation, or guilty for neglecting certain relationships. But this is just the depression talking. Staying connected to other people and taking part in social activities will make a world of difference in your mood and outlook.

Reaching out is not a sign of weakness and it won't mean you're a burden to others. Your loved ones care about you and want to help. And if you don't feel that you have anyone to turn to, it's never too late to build new friendships and improve your support network.

**How to reach out for depression support**

Look for support from people who make you feel safe and cared for. The person you talk to doesn't have to be able to fix you; they just need to be a good listener—someone who'll listen attentively and compassionately without being distracted or judging you.

Make face-time a priority. Phone calls, social media, and texting are great ways to stay in touch, but they don't replace good old-fashioned in-person quality time. The simple act of talking to someone face to face about how you feel can play a big role in relieving depression and keeping it away.

Try to keep up with social activities even if you don't feel like it. Often when you're depressed, it feels more comfortable to retreat into your shell, but being around other people will make you feel less depressed.

Find ways to support others. It's nice to receive support, but research shows you get an even bigger mood boost from providing support yourself. So find ways—both big and small—to help others: volunteer, be a listening ear for a friend, do something nice for somebody.

Care for a pet. While nothing can replace the human connection, pets can bring joy and companionship into your life and help you feel less isolated. Caring for a pet can also get you outside of yourself and give you a sense of being needed—both powerful antidotes to depression.

Join a support group for depression. Being with others dealing with depression can go a long way in reducing your sense of isolation. You can also encourage each other, give and receive advice on how to cope, and share your experiences.

**10 tips for staying connected**

Talk to one person about your feelings

Help someone else by volunteering

Have lunch or coffee with a friend

Ask a loved one to check in with you regularly

Accompany someone to the movies, a concert, or a small get-together

Call or email an old friend

Go for a walk with a workout buddy

Schedule a weekly dinner date

Meet new people by taking a class or joining a club

Confide in a clergy member, teacher, or sports coach

Tip 2: Do things that make you feel good

In order to overcome depression, you have to do things that relax and energize you. This includes following a healthy lifestyle, learning how to better manage stress, setting limits on what you're able to do, and scheduling fun activities into your day.

Do things you enjoy (or used to)

While you can't force yourself to have fun or experience pleasure, you can push yourself to do things, even when you don't feel like it. You might be surprised at how much better you feel once you're out in the world. Even if your depression doesn't lift immediately, you'll gradually feel more upbeat and energetic as you make time for fun activities.

Pick up a former hobby or a sport you used to like. Express yourself creatively through music, art, or writing. Go out with friends. Take a day trip to a museum, the mountains, or the ballpark.

Support your health

Aim for eight hours of sleep. Depression typically involves sleep problems; whether you're sleeping too little or too much, your mood suffers. Get on a better sleep schedule by learning healthy sleep habits.

Keep stress in check. Not only does stress prolong and worsen depression, but it can also trigger it. Figure out all the things in your life that stress you out, such as work overload, money problems, or unsupportive relationships, and find ways to relieve the pressure and regain control.

Practice relaxation techniques. A daily relaxation practice can help relieve symptoms of depression, reduce stress, and boost feelings of joy and well-being. Try yoga, deep breathing, progressive muscle relaxation, or meditation.

Develop a "wellness toolbox" to deal with depression

Come up with a list of things that you can do for a quick mood boost. The more "tools" for coping with depression you have, the better. Try and implement a few of these ideas each day, even if you're feeling good.

Spend some time in nature

List what you like about yourself

Read a good book

Watch a funny movie or TV show

Take a long, hot bath

Take care of a few small tasks

Play with a pet

Talk to friends or family face-to-face

Listen to music

Do something spontaneous

Tip 3: Get moving

Closeup of woman's feet striding up white, curving metal staircase

When you're depressed, just getting out of bed can seem like a daunting task, let alone working out! But exercise is a powerful depression fighter—and one of the most important tools in your recovery arsenal. Research shows that regular exercise can be as effective as medication for relieving depression symptoms. It also helps prevent relapse once you're well.

To get the most benefit, aim for at least 30 minutes of exercise per day. This doesn't have to be all at once—and it's okay to start small. A 10-minute walk can improve your mood for two hours.

Exercise is something you can do right now to boost your mood

Your fatigue will improve if you stick with it. Starting to exercise can be difficult when you're depressed and feeling exhausted. But research shows that your energy levels will improve if you keep with it. Exercise will help you to feel energized and less fatigued, not more.

Find exercises that are continuous and rhythmic. The most benefits for depression come from rhythmic exercise—such as walking, weight training, swimming, martial arts, or dancing—where you move both your arms and legs.

Add a mindfulness element, especially if your depression is rooted in unresolved trauma or fed by obsessive, negative thoughts. Focus on how your body feels as you move—such as the sensation of your feet hitting the ground, or the feeling of the wind on your skin, or the rhythm of your breathing.

Pair up with an exercise partner. Not only does working out with others enable you to spend time socializing, it can also help to keep you motivated. Try joining a running club, taking a water aerobics or dance class, seeking out tennis partners, or enrolling in a soccer or volleyball league.

Take a dog for a walk. If don't own a dog, you can volunteer to walk homeless dogs for an animal shelter or rescue group. You'll not only be helping yourself but also be helping to socialize and exercise the dogs, making them more adoptable.

Tip 4: Eat a healthy, depression-fighting diet

What you eat has a direct impact on the way you feel. Reduce your intake of foods that can adversely affect your brain and mood, such as caffeine, alcohol, trans fats, and foods with high levels of chemical preservatives or hormones (such as certain meats).

Don't skip meals. Going too long between meals can make you feel irritable and tired, so aim to eat something at least every three to four hours.

Minimize sugar and refined carbs. You may crave sugary snacks, baked goods, or comfort foods such as pasta or French fries, but these "feel-good" foods quickly lead to a crash in mood and energy. Aim to cut out as much of these foods as possible.

Boost your B vitamins. Deficiencies in B vitamins such as folic acid and B-12 can trigger depression. To get more, take a B-complex vitamin supplement or eat more citrus fruit, leafy greens, beans, chicken, and eggs.

Boost your mood with foods rich in omega-3 fatty acids. Omega-3 fatty acids play an essential role in stabilizing mood. The best sources are fatty fish such as salmon, herring, mackerel, anchovies, sardines, tuna, and some cold-water fish oil supplements.

Tip 5: Get a daily dose of sunlight

Young person wearing straw hat lying in tree-lined grass field, one bent leg resting on the other, arms folded behind head

Sunlight can help boost serotonin levels and improve your mood. Whenever possible, get outside during daylight hours and expose yourself to the sun for at least 15 minutes a day. Remove sunglasses (but never stare directly at the sun) and use sunscreen as needed.

Take a walk on your lunch break, have your coffee outside, enjoy an al fresco meal, or spend time gardening.

Double up on the benefits of sunlight by exercising outside. Try hiking, walking in a local park, or playing golf or tennis with a friend.

Increase the amount of natural light in your home and workplace by opening blinds and drapes and sitting near windows.

If you live somewhere with little winter sunshine, try using a light therapy box.

Dealing with the winter blues

For some people, the reduced daylight hours of winter lead to a form of depression known as seasonal affective disorder (SAD). SAD can make you feel like a completely different person to who you are in the summer: hopeless, sad, tense, or stressed, with no interest in friends or activities you normally love. No matter how hopeless you feel, though, there are plenty of things you can do to keep your mood stable throughout the year.

Tip 6: Challenge negative thinking

Do you feel like you're powerless or weak? That bad things happen and there's not much you can do about it? That your situation is hopeless? Depression puts a negative spin on everything, including the way you see yourself and your expectations for the future.

When these types of thoughts overwhelm you, it's important to remember that this is a symptom of your depression and these irrational, pessimistic attitudes—known as cognitive distortions—aren't realistic.

When you really examine them they don't hold up. But even so, they can be tough to give up. You can't break out of this pessimistic mind frame by telling yourself to "just think positive." Often, it's part of a lifelong pattern of thinking that's become so automatic you're not even completely aware of it. Rather, the trick is to identify the type of negative thoughts that are fueling your depression, and replace them with a more balanced way of thinking.

Negative, unrealistic ways of thinking that fuel depression

All-or-nothing thinking – Looking at things in black-or-white categories, with no middle ground ("If everything is not perfect, I'm a total failure.")

Overgeneralization – Generalizing from a single negative experience, expecting it to hold true forever ("I had a bad date, I'll never find anyone.")

The mental filter – Ignoring positive events and focusing on the negative. Noticing the one thing that went wrong, rather than all the things that went right. ("I got the last question on the test wrong. I'm an idiot.")

Diminishing the positive – Coming up with reasons why positive events don't count ("She said she had a good time on our date, but I think she was just being nice."

Jumping to conclusions – Making negative interpretations without actual evidence. You act like a mind reader ("He must think I'm pathetic") or a fortune teller ("I'll be stuck in this dead-end job forever.")

Emotional reasoning – Believing that the way you feel reflects reality ("I feel like such a loser. Everyone must be laughing at me!")

'Shoulds' and 'should-nots' – Holding yourself to a strict list of what you should and shouldn't do, and beating yourself up if you don't live up to your rules. ("I should never have interviewed for that job. I'm an idiot for thinking I could get it.")

Labeling – Classifying yourself based on mistakes and perceived shortcomings ("I'm a failure; an idiot; a loser.")

Put your thoughts on the witness stand

Once you identify the destructive thoughts patterns that contribute to your depression, you can start to challenge them with questions such as:

"What's the evidence that this thought is true? Not true?"

"What would I tell a friend who had this thought?"

"Is there another way of looking at the situation or an alternate explanation?"

"How might I look at this situation if I didn't have depression?"

As you cross-examine your negative thoughts, you may be surprised at how quickly they crumble. In the process, you'll develop a more balanced perspective and help to relieve your depression.

When to get professional help for depression

If you've taken self-help steps and made positive lifestyle changes and still find your depression getting worse, seek professional help. Needing additional help doesn't mean you're weak.

Sometimes the negative thinking in depression can make you feel like you're a lost cause, but depression can be treated and you can feel better!

Don't forget about these self-help tips, though. Even if you're receiving professional help, these tips can be part of your treatment plan, speeding your recovery and preventing depression from returning.

# 3.PRACTICE THESE SKILLS EVERY DAY

I recommend doing many — if not all — of the following coping skills and techniques once a day when experiencing depression. It's important to know you probably won't be motivated to do any of them at first because depression frequently saps motivation. In other words, know that it's normal to feel unmotivated until you're halfway done.

### *1. Meaning:*

Find small ways to be of service to others.

Find personal meaning by serving something larger than yourself. Remember service doesn't have to be big to count. Consider this, "Success, like happiness, cannot be pursued; it must ensue… as the unintended side effect of one's personal dedication to a course greater than oneself." – Viktor E. Frankl, Man's Search for Meaning

### *2. Your goals:*

Find workable goals that give you a sense of accomplishment.

Most people feel guilty when talking about goals because they set unreasonable or unworkable goals. A goal is workable if it's:

Something you can control (i.e., it doesn't depend on others)

Manageable (i.e., not overwhelming)

Realistic for you (not for someone else)

Measurable (i.e., you know whether or not it is done or getting done)

If something goes wrong with your goal, adopt a "what can I learn from this?" attitude (versus a judgmental, "this is why I'm horrible" attitude).

Also, be careful when comparing your progress with others. We usually compare our biggest weakness with another person's biggest strength. This is unfair (and usually not accurate anyhow).

### *3. Pleasant Events:*

Schedule pleasant activities or events.

Don't wait for yourself to be "in the mood." For example, give yourself permission for a 30-minute "vacation" or schedule a healthy hobby every day. Just remember to do these activities with the right attitude (see Engagement).

Also, practice gratitude — take time to notice what went well today, not just what went wrong. Consider keeping a gratitude journal. Know that being grateful for your blessings doesn't mean you have to discount your problems.

### *4. Engagement:*

Stay in the present.

This practice is sometimes called mindfulness. As best you can, during activities try not to be in your head with self-judgment. You may not be able to turn off the self-judgment, but you can notice it and bring yourself gently back to the present.

Research shows that people with higher self-compassion also have higher self-worth or self-confidence.

**Exercise 1: How would you treat a friend?**

Please take out a sheet of paper and answer the following questions:

First, think about times when a close friend feels really bad about him or herself or is really struggling in some way. How would you respond to your friend in this situation (especially when you're at your best)? Please write down what you typically do, what you say, and note the tone in which you typically talk to your friends.

Now think about times when you feel bad about yourself or are struggling. How do you typically respond to yourself in these situations? Please write down what you typically do, what you say, and note the tone in which you talk to yourself.

Did you notice a difference? If so, ask yourself why. What factors or fears come into play that lead you to treat yourself and others so differently?

Please write down how you think things might change if you responded to yourself in the same way you typically respond to a close friend when you're suffering.

**Exercise 2: Self-Compassion Break**

Think of a situation in your life that is difficult, that is causing you stress. Call the situation to mind, and see if you can actually feel the stress and emotional discomfort in your body.

Now, say to yourself:

1. This is a moment of suffering

That's mindfulness. Other options include:

- This hurts.
- Ouch.
- This is stress.

2. Suffering is a part of life

That's common humanity. Other options include:

- Other people feel this way.
- I'm not alone.
- We all struggle in our lives.

Now, put your hands over your heart, feel the warmth of your hands and the gentle touch of your hands on your chest. Or adopt the soothing touch you discovered felt right for you.

Say to yourself:

3. May I be kind to myself

You can also ask yourself, "What do I need to hear right now to express kindness to myself?" Is there a phrase that speaks to you in your particular situation, such as:

- May I give myself the compassion that I need
- May I learn to accept myself as I am
- May I forgive myself
- May I be strong.
- May I be patient

**Exercise 3: Exploring self-compassion through writing**

Part One: Which imperfections make you feel inadequate?

Everybody has something about themselves that they don't like; something that causes them to feel shame, to feel insecure, or not "good enough." It is the human condition to be imperfect, and feelings of failure and inadequacy are part of the experience of living a human life.

Try writing about an issue you have that tends to make you feel inadequate or bad about yourself (physical appearance, work or relationship issues…)

What emotions come up for you when you think about this aspect of yourself? Try to just feel your emotions exactly as they are – no more, no less – and then write about them.

Part Two: Write a letter to yourself from the perspective of an unconditionally loving imaginary friend

Now think about an imaginary friend who is unconditionally loving, accepting, kind and compassionate. Imagine that this friend can see all your strengths and all your weaknesses, including the aspect of yourself you have just been writing about.

Reflect upon what this friend feels towards you, and how you are loved and accepted exactly as you are, with all your very human imperfections.

This friend recognizes the limits of human nature, and is kind and forgiving towards you. In his/her great wisdom this friend understands your life history and the millions of things that have happened in your life to create you as you are in this moment.

Your particular inadequacy is connected to so many things you didn't necessarily choose: your genes, your family history, life circumstances – things that were outside of your control.

Write a letter to yourself from the perspective of this imaginary friend – focusing on the perceived inadequacy you tend to judge yourself for.

What would this friend say to you about your "flaw" from the perspective of unlimited compassion? How would this friend convey the deep compassion he/she feels for you, especially for the pain you feel when you judge yourself so harshly?

What would this friend write in order to remind you that you are only human, that all people have both strengths and weaknesses?

And if you think this friend would suggest possible changes you should make, how would these suggestions embody feelings of unconditional understanding and compassion? As you write to yourself from the perspective of this imaginary friend, try to infuse your letter with a strong sense of his/her acceptance, kindness, caring, and desire for your health and happiness.

Part Three: Feel the compassion as it soothes and comforts you

After writing the letter, put it down for a little while. Then come back and read it again, really letting the words sink in. Feel the compassion as it pours into you, soothing and comforting you like a cool breeze on a hot day.

Love, connection and acceptance are your birthright. To claim them you need only look within yourself.

**Exercise 4: Supportive Touch**

One easy way to care for and comfort yourself when you're feeling badly is to give yourself supportive touch. Touch activates the care system and the parasympathetic nervous system to help us calm down and feel safe.

It may feel awkward or embarrassing at first, but your body doesn't know that. It just responds to the physical gesture of warmth and care, just as a baby responds to being cuddled in its mother's arms.

Our skin is an incredibly sensitive organ. Research indicates that physical touch releases oxytocin, provides a sense of security, soothes distressing emotions, and calms cardiovascular stress. So why not try it?

You might like to try putting your hand on your body during difficult periods several times a day for a period of at least a week.

Hand-on-Heart

When you notice you're under stress, take 2-3 deep, satisfying breaths.

Gently place your hand over your heart, feeling the gentle pressure and warmth of your hand. If you wish, place both hands on your chest, noticing the difference between one and two hands.

Feel the touch of you hand on your chest. If you wish, you could make small circles with your hand on your chest.

Feel the natural rising and falling of your chest as you breathe in and as you breathe out.

Linger with the feeling for as long as you like.

Some people feel uneasy putting a hand over the heart. Feel free to explore where on your body a gentle touch is actually soothing. Some other possibilities are:

One hand on your cheek

Cradling your face in your hands

Gently stroking your arms

Crossing your arms and giving a gentle squeeze

Gently rubbing your chest, or using circular movements

Hand on your abdomen

One hand on your abdomen and one over heart

Cupping one hand in the other in your lap

Hopefully you'll start to develop the habit of physically comforting yourself when needed, taking full advantage of this surprisingly simple and straightforward way to be kind to ourselves.

**Exercise 5: Changing your critical self-talk**

This exercise should be done over several weeks and will eventually form the blueprint for changing how you relate to yourself long-term. Some people find it useful to work on their inner critic by writing in a journal.

Others are more comfortable doing it via internal dialogues. If you are someone who likes to write things down and revisit them later, journaling can be an excellent tool for transformation.

If you are someone (like me) who never manages to be consistent with a journal, then do whatever works for you. You can speak aloud to yourself, or think silently.

The first step towards changing the way to treat yourself is to notice when you are being self-critical. It may be that – like many of us — your self-critical voice is so common for you that you don't even notice when it is present.

Whenever you're feeling bad about something, think about what you've just said to yourself. Try to be as accurate as possible, noting your inner speech verbatim.

What words do you actually use when you're self-critical? Are there key phrases that come up over and over again? What is the tone of your voice – harsh, cold, angry?

Does the voice remind you of any one in your past who was critical of you? You want to be able to get to know the inner self-critic very well, and to become aware of when your inner judge is active.

For instance, if you've just eaten half a box of Oreo's, does your inner voice say something like "you're so disgusting," "you make me sick," and so on? Really try to get a clear sense of how you talk to yourself.

Make an active effort to soften the self-critical voice, but do so with compassion rather than self-judgment (i.e., don't say "you're such a bitch" to your inner critic!). Say something like "I know you're worried about me and feel unsafe, but you are causing me unnecessary pain. Could you let my inner compassionate self say a few words now?"

Reframe the observations made by your inner critic in a friendly, positive way. If you're having trouble thinking of what words to use, you might want to imagine what a very compassionate friend would say to you in this situation.

It might help to use a term of endearment that strengthens expressed feelings of warmth and care (but only if it feels natural rather than schmaltzy.)

For instance, you can say something like "Darling, I know you ate that bag of cookies because you're feeling really sad right now and you thought it would cheer you up. But you feel even worse and are not feeling good in your body.

I want you to be happy, so why don't you take a long walk so you feel better?" While engaging in this supportive self-talk, you might want to try gently stroking your arm, or holding your face tenderly in your hands (as long as no one's looking). Physical gestures of warmth can tap into the caregiving system even if you're having trouble calling up emotions of kindness at first, releasing oxytocin that will help change your bio-chemistry. The important thing is that you start acting kindly, and feelings of true warmth and caring will eventually follow.

**Exercise 6: Self-Compassion Journal**

Try keeping a daily self-compassion journal for one week (or longer if you like.) Journaling is an effective way to express emotions, and has been found to enhance both mental and physical well-being.

At some point during the evening when you have a few quiet moments, review the day's events. In your journal, write down anything that you felt bad about, anything you judged yourself for, or any difficult experience that caused you pain. (For instance, perhaps you got angry at a waitress at lunch because she took forever to bring the check.

You made a rude comment and stormed off without leaving a tip. Afterwards, you felt ashamed and embarrassed.) For each event, use mindfulness, a sense of common humanity, and kindness to process the event in a more self-compassionate way.

Mindfulness

This will mainly involve bring awareness to the painful emotions that arose due to your self-judgment or difficult circumstances. Write about how you felt: sad, ashamed, frightened, stressed, and so on. As you write, try to be accepting and non-judgmental of your experience, not belittling it nor making it overly dramatic. (For example, "I was frustrated because she was being so slow. I got angry, over-reacted, and felt foolish afterwards.")

Common Humanity

Write down the ways in which your experience was connected to the larger human experience. This might include acknowledging that being human means being imperfect, and that all people have these sorts of painful experiences.

("Everyone over-reacts sometimes, it's only human.") You might also want to think about the various causes and conditions underlying the painful event. ("My frustration was exacerbated by the fact that I was late for my doctor's appointment across town and there was a lot of traffic that day. If the circumstances had been different my reaction probably would have been different.")

Self-Kindness

Write yourself some kind, understanding, words of comfort. Let yourself know that you care about yourself, adopting a gentle, reassuring tone.

(It's okay. You messed up but it wasn't the end of the world. I understand how frustrated you were and you just lost it. Maybe you can try being extra patient and generous to any wait-staff this week…")

Practicing the three components of self-compassion with this writing exercise will help organize your thoughts and emotions, while helping to encode them in your memory. If you keep a journal regularly, your self-compassion practice will become even stronger and translate more easily into daily life.

**Exercise 7: Identifying what we really want**

Think about the ways that you use self-criticism as a motivator. Is there any personal trait that you criticize yourself for having (too overweight, too lazy, too impulsive, etc.) because you think being hard on yourself will help you change?

If so, first try to get in touch with the emotional pain that your self-criticism causes, giving yourself compassion for the experience of feeling so judged.

Next, see if you can think of a kinder, more caring way to motivate yourself to make a change if needed. What language would a wise and nurturing friend, parent, teacher, or mentor use to gently point out how your behavior is unproductive, while simultaneously encouraging you to do something different. What is the most supportive message you can think of that's in line with your underlying wish to be healthy and happy?

Every time you catch yourself being judgmental about your unwanted trait in the future, first notice the pain of your self-judgment and give yourself compassion.

Then try to reframe your inner dialogue so that it is more encouraging and supportive. Remember that if you really want to motivate yourself, love is more powerful than fear

**Exercise 8: Taking care of the caregiver**

If you work in a care-giving profession (and that certainly includes being a family member!), you'll need to recharge your batteries so you have enough energy available to give to others. Give yourself permission to meet your own needs, recognizing that this will not only enhance your quality of life, it will also enhance your ability to be there for those that rely on you. For instance, you might listen to relaxing music, take a yoga class, hang out with a friend for an evening, or get a massage.

Of course, sometime our time is limited and we aren't able to take care of ourselves as much as we'd like. Also, one limitation of self-care strategies is that they're "off the job," and can't be done while you're actually caregiving.

Thus, it's important to also engage in "on the job" self care. When you're feeling stressed or overwhelmed when with the person you're caring for, you might try giving yourself soothing words of support (for example "I know this is hard right now, and it's only natural you're feeling so stressed. I'm here for you.").

Or else you might try using soothing touch or the self-compassion break. This will allow you to keep your heart open, and help you care for and nurture yourself at the same time you're caring for and nurturing others.

### 5. *Exercise:*

And, eat right too.

Doing moderate exercise about five times a week (30 minutes a pop) can dramatically help your mood. Moderate exercise is a level of activity where it is difficult to sing from your diaphragm while doing it. Also pay attention to how the type of food or drink you're eating influences your mood. You don't have to do fad diets, but anyone will be depressed if they frequently binge on carbs, junk food, and energy drinks. Remember the virtue of moderation.

### *6. Relationships*:

Focus on people who lift you up.

Interact frequently with others that bring you up (not people that bring you down). While it's OK to have some alone time, find a balance and don't isolate yourself or the depression will linger.

### *7. Sleep Regularly:*

Try to keep a regular sleep schedule.

Keep a balance with not too little and not too much sleep. Staying up late one night and then sleeping in excessively the next day is a sure-fire way to feed depression. Also, don't try to solve problems late at night when your brain is half-asleep.

As you practice these coping skills, know that you're on the path to overcoming depression

In contrast, depression tends to linger when patients make up a reason why they can't do these things. No matter what medication you're taking, doing several of these activities every day — especially when you don't feel like it — is vital to the treatment of depression.

These positive coping skills may take time and practice, but if we don't take the time to be well now, the periods of "unwellness" may be forced upon us later.

# ABOUT THE AUTHOR

I am Chirstopher Carlson. I'm a student in university. I've compiled a great list here and I've excited they're all in the one spot. I hope you enjoy it as much as I enjoyed making it!

When you finish this book it would be amazing if you could leave a review for me as it'd mean the world.

Thanks so much for reading by my little corner.

Hope you enjoy the book!

www.ingramcontent.com/pod-product-compliance
Lightning Source LLC
LaVergne TN
LVHW040934150826
845672LV00007B/2365

* 9 7 9 8 4 6 4 3 1 3 5 1 4 *